Wise or Otherwise

Lou Wise

ISBN: 061593417X
ISBN-13: 978-0615934174

Lou Wise

.

DEDICATION

To all I have known---
You were my inspiration, my material, my life

Lou Wise

CONTENTS

1 INTRODUCTIONS

How you doin? My name is Lou Wise and I drink. A lot. The reason I tell you this is because in my years of being drunk in bars, out of bars, in the street, under cars, and around other drunks, I have learned a lot. It is my intention here to provide you with a unique, perhaps warped, view of the world. Why do I want to do this? Because I can; you bought the book, apparently you want to hear what I have to say.

I am not an eloquent writer; I do not pretend to have a mastery of the written language. I also have no idea where this book is going. I'm gonna tell you some stories. Some will have a moral, some will enlighten you, and some are just damn funny. Judge for yourself which is which.

Now most but not all of these stories are mine and mine alone. I have borrowed a few from friends, from relatives, from drunk bastards sitting alone at a bar. If you happen to be one of my friends, enemies, or acquaintances of which I have stolen stories from—I mean borrowed stories from, thank you—I hope I have done your stories justice. And please, don't kick my ass.

So as not to confuse the reader, my publisher (prick) wants me to explain how I wrote this book. I guess he feels that it will make more sense if you understand my thought process or lack thereof while I was writing.

This book was originally recorded. One night I had been drinking, notice a pattern, and found myself in Walmart. Now I love Walmart at two in the morning, it's so cool. On this particular trip, I decided to buy a micro-cassette recorder. I don't know why I bought it, it was like 88 cents or something. You know their strange pricing system. You know Walmart; you know Walmart drunk, admit it, you do. Enough said.

So I began talking, bitching, into this little 88 cent recorder. I started talking about life, love, sex, beer, and a host of other pointless things. I filled tons of those little tapes with nonsense. Then one day I'm hanging out with this guy Grec, we start talking and he notices that I have this little recorder with me. He asks me about it and I tell him I was drunk, in Walmart, 88 cents, blah, blah, blah.

Eventually this guy convinces me to let him hear some of my tapes. He loves them and says we should make a book out of the stories on the tapes. At first I think he is trying to pick me up. It's this skinny little, well dressed, well groomed guy… talking to me in a bar; what would you think? But then I realize he is simply a money hungry bastard who thinks he can make a dime off of me. (I was right on both accounts.)

Now I don't know shit about writing a book, but I tried, and it sucked. I tried again, and it still sucked. So I eventually I go back to this guy and say "it ain't gonna work, I'm retarded. I can't write a book, let alone see which keys I'm hitting." (If I haven't mentioned it before, I drink a lot.)

My friend isn't deterred, but like the good man he is (bullshit! I just say that 'cause he's paying the bills), he suggests we go out and have a drink. After about two-thirds of a bottle of Johnny Red, he realizes why he likes the stories. He tells me that it wasn't just the stories, it was how they were told and why they were told that was interesting to him. (Apparently, babbling while drunk appeals to him.) He then suggests that I take the tapes play them back and transcribe them, verbatim, onto paper. After I found a dictionary and figured out what verbatim meant, I agreed.

So Grec, and other listeners, I mean readers, (hell even the intro was recorded originally) here is word for word what I transcribed verbatim (I love that word now) from those tapes. I must warn you though, at times I may go off on a tangent, other times I might break out in song, or I may just describe for pages how great the beer tastes. Mmmmm…beer, so good, so cold, so…I digress.

Now, the following chapters are not exactly verbatim. (I really like that word!) I believe Grec, my publisher, has gotten his hands on it and may have changed, toned down, and otherwise fucked my stories up. But hopefully, knowing Grec, he had a whole bunch of drinks first, and could barely even see, let alone use his computer, and didn't screw me too bad (though I still think he wants to).

But like any good publisher Grec wants to cover his ass, so he has had me insert the next few lines as a precaution to any future litigation. (Had to look that one up too).

First any depiction of places, persons living or dead, is purely coincidental. (Bullshit, if you're in this book you know who you are). Also, we—*I* do not condone the abuse of alcohol, especially by those who are under the legal age of consumption (unless they're cute), which is twenty-one. And last but not least I would personally like to apologize to Jimmy Buffett. I am a huge Parrothead and at times in this book will quote, or even sing many a line from Buffett. Mr. Buffett, it is all in good fun sir, please do not sue us. By the way you rock Jimmy!!! (Long live the Conch Republic!)

I would also encourage the reader not to try and figure out who is who in this book. Like I said some of these stories are my stories, some are the stories of others, and some my publisher (prick) has edited, changed, and thoroughly fucked beyond all recognition. Some of these stories are purely fiction. (Yeah right, I just have to say that as to not get sued.)

I would like, if I may, to set down a few rules to abide by before reading this book. First and foremost, do not take everything I say seriously.

Though I mean just about everything I write, these are my views, my views alone, my views while under the influence of alcohol. They may be a little
...a little... let's just say a little bit off at times. So don't go become a raging alcoholic just because I think it is a good idea. And I do.

Also, I may claim to have all the answers, but I don't. I mean I think I do, but so do most people. My conclusions work for me. They may work for you. They may not. You be the judge. Just keep in mind that I am usually right.

Secondly, if you are of the legal drinking age, have a few drinks while you read my book. It will make the whole experience way more enjoyable. Trust me I wrote this book. *I* wouldn't even read it sober. In fact I think I will make this book the first ever interactive literary drinking game. Take that, Shakespeare! (This will so get us sued.)

Here are the rules of the game. Randomly throughout the book you will see the word "***Drink***". Whenever you see this word, have a sip. Now, in order to play you must be prepared, so have some beer, a mixed drink, whatever it is you like to imbibe, sitting next to you. Go now, get a drink, I wouldn't want you to have to interrupt the wonderful flow of this book in order to get a drink. So everyone stop reading, go to the fridge, side bar, local pub and get something. Don't worry, I'll wait; I'll be right here when you get back.

For those of you not playing along (pussy) just ignore the word "Drink" which will appear randomly throughout the book. You can just sit there and realize how pathetic you are. I just want you to know that everyone else is having fun and you're not. And you're an ass-clit.

For those of you playing along, you kick ass; give me a call, send me an e-mail, you're cool, and you owe me a "***Drink***". Now that makes two, or is it three? This is gonna be so much fun.

Like I said I drink too much, other people learn things when I drink; which is good for you because I'm drinking now, so you will learn.

"Never Trust A Man Who Doesn't Drink"
----- Unknown

2 ALCOHOL

Never trust a man who doesn't drink. This phrase hangs on a faded wood sign in my favorite bar. (I love you Trish!) I believe whole-heartedly in this phrase, and for a few good reasons. One being that there is really no good reason not to drink. Yeah, yeah, yeah, I hear those of you who are all health conscious and shit, saying it's bad for you.

So what! What today won't kill you? There's skin cancer, which comes from the sun. The sun, you know, the bright star that is the reason that this planet has the ability to even sustain life, yeah, you know what I'm talking about, may give you skin cancer. I guess we just need to get rid of the sun; it's bad for you.

There is also lung cancer, cancer from cell phones, cancer from genetically engineered foods, cancer from holes in the ozone layer, terrorism, hell I could slip next time I step in the shower and die. Don't even try to give me that health reason bullshit.

Plus, I believe that I read somewhere that drinking one glass of red wine a day helps prevent heart disease. Hell, if one glass a day helps prevent heart disease, then one bottle a day should truly cure it. Right? ***"Drink"***
Right!

The second reason that you should drink is that it makes life so much more fun. There are many activities in life that would totally suck if it were not for the consumption of alcohol. In fact, I think the next chapter of this book should list all the activities in life that are made better by drinking. I wonder if the next chapter will be about that? Well let's read on and find out. ***"Drink"***

The third reason why you should never trust a man/woman (I'm being politically correct) who doesn't drink is because he/she is hiding something. Those of us who are well versed in the world of drinking know certain things. We all know that there are a few secrets, a few stories that we would never tell anyone unless we had a few drinks in us. For instance, this book. Sober, this book would never have happened. Even though I wanted to, I needed to be drunk to write it.

I'm sure that by the end of this book I will have drank so much that I will have told you every embarrassing story I have and some that my friends have. (Sorry guys.) Many people who don't drink are afraid of this.
They're afraid that they will lose control. They are afraid that they may do or say something that they wouldn't normally do unless they were drunk.

This is a load of shit! Alcohol does not make us do anything. Anything! One more time!
Anything!

Everything we do drunk we secretly want to do sober, but we just, for whatever reason, don't. Once again, this book for example.

Believe me, every stupid, embarrassing story that we tell when we are drunk, we really want to tell when we are sober, we are just a bit scared. Every person we tell off because they're an asshole, well you know what? They are assholes when we're sober as well. Trust me, just because

you think and say
someone is an asshole when you are drunk, sobriety does
not make him or her any less an asshole. Let me explain.

Girls, when you get drunk and sleep with half the
football team guess what? It's not the booze; somewhere
deep down inside, you wanted to. And guys, same goes for
us.

The next morning when you wake up next to the girl
with the hairy lip and lazy eye, the one which your friends
will never let you live down, the
one they fuck with you so hard about, and the same one you
have to go to a shrink for years just to put up with their
tormenting for? Yeah, you know who I'm talking about, it
wasn't the beer dude, you had a hard-on for a fat, hairy chick,
with a lazy eye... admit it, you did. *"Drink"*

The next reason that you should never trust a man or
woman who doesn't drink is well, why would you hang out
with someone who doesn't? I
mean it has got to be a really fucking boring night, right?
What are you supposed to do with them, sit there and stare at
each other? You could go to dinner I guess, but what would
you drink, soda?

Could you imagine going out to a fine Italian restaurant
and not drinking? Picture this: you sit down, order your fried
calamari appetizer, your veal parmesan, and do not enjoy a fine
bottle of Chianti. It's sacrilegious! Might as well order a
McDouble and a large fry to go with your delicious "diet
Coke."

Perhaps you could go to the movies; unfortunately most
movies suck. Try and sit through the "Aviator" and not crave a
drink. (Whoever wrote and/or directed that movie, please don't
sue me.)

You could go to a library, but they close early. And most
librarians have a funny sort of smell about them. Don't forget,
ladies and gents, most of the places you pick a person up at are
bars. I guess my point is there are just times when you need to
go to the local pub and order yourself a pint.
Here's an example: What happens if your friend or your date
happens to be really boring? Are you going to sit there in

silence, or worse, sit there and listen to them ramble on and on about pointless shit that you don't and never will care about sober? Hear them bitch about politics, about religion, views you probably disagree with, and enjoy yourself? Fuck no. You want to be able to drink during these painful episodes. Trust me, you need to do something before you have sex with them.

"Never trust a man who doesn't drink." I would love to meet the man who came up with this very astute, very insightful quote. I wish I would have been the one who said that. But since I'm not, I would like to offer my very own insightful quote. Here it goes: "Never trust a woman who doesn't drink…They're boring as hell! And a lot less easy to convince to have sex with you." (There's some great English for you.)

"Some people drink, Some people don't, Some people think and some people won't"
----- Dave Matthews Band

3 I LOVE TO DRINK

I love to drink. It has to be my favorite pastime. Just about every activity is made more enjoyable by drinking. Here are a few examples:

Bowling: Could you imagine bowling without drinking beer? I know

I can't. Yes, we all did it when we were in middle school, but it sucked. Bowling is not a sport, and fuck you if you think it is. Bowling is something to do while you sit inside and drink. Shit, some bars even have bowling video games in them. When a bar promotes bowling, you know it has to be made better by alcohol.

Dancing: Girls, you may disagree, but guys, you have my back on this, there is no way in hell I'm getting on a dance floor unless I am thoroughly blasted. At least then I don't realize how bad, uncoordinated, gangly, and pathetic I look.

Shit, after a few rounds, I look hot when I dance. By that I mean I'm really embarrassing, I just don't realize it. And that is ok.

Sex: Enough said. There would be no way in the world I would ever get laid if it weren't for beer. Plus, there has been many a time when I would have gone home to sleep alone had that last drink or three not made the girl at the end of the bar with the hairy lip look really good. *"Why don't we get drunk and screw?"* Thanks for that Jimmy. You too, Johnny, Jack and Jose.

The Olympics: What a fucking sheep show that is. You wait four years to see some people who have way too much time on their hands run around in circles, see who can jump farther, or ride down a big ass ice cube on a sled. Try and sit through that disappointment sober. Hell where's my beer? Just thinking about it makes me want to drink. *"Drink"*

Driving: Driving is really fun drunk. Just kidding. There is a reason God invented cabs.

Music: Most music is good with or without a drink, but you really enjoy music after a few. You can pop in a CD sober, sit there, move your head, tap your foot, perhaps even sing a few lines. But put on the same song when you have a good buzz, well shit, next thing you know you're jumping up on the couch, dancing around, and shouting the words into your beer bottle.

Cards: Playing cards is fun, but most of the time you sit there and drink while you play. Also, there are so many really cool drinking games you can play with cards. And just remember, it's really hard to get a girl to play strip poker, strip blackjack, strip pinochle, hell strip anything when they are sober. Trust me, I once dated a Mormon chick. That was a load of fun.

Flying: Flying has to be one of the most frustrating activities on the planet. It's ranked right up there with brushing your teeth with your left hand. The only way to make flying even slightly bearable is to drink. Drink at the airport, drink on the plane, drink during your layover. And by the way, they make the best Bloody Mary's at the airport. Hell, even some of the pilots drink.

Pool: Let's face it pool is a great game. Any game where you get to use your stick and put balls in a hole has got to be good. ***"Drink"*** But we all know that having a few beers while "*sinking your balls*" makes the game so much more fun.

This Book: This book sucks sober. Trust me, I had to be drunk just to write it.

Lou Wise

4 ALCOHOL PART TWO

Alcohol is not the answer to every problem; hell it's not the answer to any problem. Well, unless sobriety is your problem. Then I guess alcohol really is the answer. Think about that one.

Though alcohol may not be a cure for most problems it will help dull the pain and, more importantly, help you get by. Don't believe me? Here try this little exercise.

Step One: Look around you; do you see something hard, something solid? Yes. Good, now punch it. Hit it as hard as you fucking can! Don't be a bitch, hit the shit out of it! Good! I bet that didn't feel very good.

Step Two: Grab a drink, a drink that should already be sitting next to you. Now drink it. ***"Drink"*** In a few minutes the pain in your hand will go away. If not have another drink. ***"Drink"*** Eventually you will no longer feel any pain.

God, I really hope none of you tried that experiment. I would really have to question the intelligence of my readers if too many of you tried that. Fuck, what am I talking about, you bought this book; I already question your intelligence. Just kidding, you're the reason I can afford the good booze.

Alcohol is good. Alcohol is great. Alcohol is astonishing. Alcohol is amazing. Alcohol is wonderful. Alcohol is superb. Alcohol is outstanding. Alcohol is exceptional. Alcohol is incomparable. (I love my thesaurus.)

Alcohol: it comes in so many forms, so many different forms that we each have an opportunity to enjoy it. Some of us, myself included, will drink anything. I'll drink beer, wine, straight liquor, shots, mixed drinks, and the list goes on. There are some of you who are straight beer drinkers. Others like only girly, milky, fruity tasting drinks.

Hell even the stuck up, rich snobs who would never stoop to the level of beer still like getting a nice buzz with a hundred dollar bottle of wine or champagne. Whatever your particular taste is, alcohol is there for you. Alcohol: the friend who will never leave you.

We all drink for different reasons, and those reasons constantly change. At times we drink to relieve stress. Other times we drink to loosen up, to become more personable. Some of us drink because we like, perhaps even love, the taste of alcohol. I know I do. *"Drink"*

Some of us drink because we want to feel that magical buzz that alcohol gives us. At times we may drink to fit in. I think, no, I know most of us drink to have an excuse. Like I've said before, we do not do anything drunk that we wouldn't do sober. But, if we're drunk, we suddenly have an excuse for our behavior.

For example, I didn't want to sleep with your sister; I was drunk. Or, that sheep was willing. "*Bahhh*" means "yes" in my book.

Hey girls, here's one for you: you don't like women, you only did it once, 'cause you were drunk. Sure, right. Your secret is safe with me. And the few hundred thousand people who have bought this book.

5 WOMEN AND LOVE

God, before I touch on this topic, I really need to get a good buzz on. ***"Drink"*** I need to feel that sweet, cool sensation that comes with alcohol before I jump into this topic. ***"Drink"*** There, I feel the dulling of the senses, the clouding of judgment, the loosening of lips. ***"Drink"*** Hang in there, just one more swallow of this magical drink of the gods. ***"Drink"*** OK, I'm good now.

Love and relationships are the most frustrating thing in the world. They are about as frustrating as trying to brush your teeth with your left hand. (I know I have said that before, but I use the phrase again to reiterate my point.)

But relationships are what we all strive for. Think about it, most of us want to be rich, have nice houses, nice cars, ect, ect. Why do we do this? It's simple: it's because we want to impress people.

Most importantly, we want to impress members of the
opposite sex
(or the same sex, depending on your particular taste). Do you
really care if your "boys" think you drive a really hot car? Fuck
no! You want the hot car to impress the ladies. And if you
disagree with me, you are a fucking liar.
Capital "L," small "i," small "a," small "r," period!"

This is a very difficult topic to write about, and there
are a multitude of reasons for it. I'll spare you the full list
and only explain a few. The first is that everyone is looking
for different things out of a relationship. Some of us want
companionship. We think, "It would be nice to be able to
sit here with someone and talk, to share, to have someone to
tell about my day, to take on a nice long walk." Some of us
need companionship, almost to the point that we can't
function without it. We think, " Oh shit! I can't be alone!
What will I do? I need someone, anyone."

Some of the ladies out there want a man to take care
of them. They think, "Isn't this great? I don't have to
work, and I get whatever I want!"

Some of the ladies are in desperate need for a man
to take care of them and their kids. They think, "Isn't this
great? I have someone who will take care of and look out
for me and my kids!"

Some of us use relationships as a status symbol. We
like to show off how hot, how attractive our significant
other is. Ladies think, " Look at what my man bought me.
This is a two hundred dollar purse. Don't you wish your
man bought you shit like this?"

The guys think, "Check out my new piece of ass.
Doesn't she look great? I know you all want a piece of this.
Don't you wish your girl looked like this?"

Some of us just want sex. Straight up we just want sex.
We think, "I want to get off, I need to get
off, better find somebody." Some of us want a relationship
so we can have constant sex. We think, "I'm lazy, finding a
hookup every time I want sex is just too much work. I want
to find someone so I can get laid whenever I want with as
little effort as possible."

And there are dozens more reasons out there why we seek companionship. Which one is right? The answer is none. They are simply different motivating factors that we all have to reach the same goal. What goal is that? Fuck, I don't know. But it usually has to do with getting laid.

The second reason that this sucks to talk about is that it involves feelings. Yes, yes, I know I have already bitched, complained, and passionately discussed my love of drinking. But this, this is different. With love, it is so much more complicated. For most of us, it has to do with control. It's good to control some things in life, that's why I love alcohol so much. I can control it. (Well to some extent I can.) I can choose whether I pick up the glass sitting next to me or not. Hell, I want to pick it up. *__"Drink"__* Damn, that was good.

This isn't the way relationships should work. In a good--no, scratch that, --in a great relationship, no one has control. That is the scariest and hardest thing to deal with in relationships.

I'm sure we have all been in relationships where we were in control. We knew how the relationship was going to go. There was going to be zero surprises. We knew when and if they were going to end. The other person involved was so committed, so complacent that we could control the course of the relationship.

You know what, these relationships are fun, they are easy, but we all know they are not right. And I don't know why that is. Common sense should tell you that this relationship should be good. It's not.

I, and perhaps I'm wrong, believe that the best relationships, the healthiest are the ones where no one has that control. For some reason having the fear that this relationship could end at any moment, that she could up and leave, --or for that matter so could I, --makes me work harder.

It makes me appreciate the relationship more. Knowing that the reason we are together is not because I have control, not because she has control, and knowing that every day we spend together is because we both want to be, is beautiful to me. Shit, maybe I'm just crazy and a sadist. Who knows?

Finding a relationship like that is hard. Those are the ones where you take the most risk. Speaking from experience, and I know many of you will agree with this, we have been in relationships simply because they were easy, they were fun. We got whatever we wanted out of them. (Whatever that may have been.)

If these relationships ended, well, we weren't going to lose much sleep over them. The relationships where you don't want them to end, the ones where you have invested your time, effort, and not wanting to sound like some pathetic hippie, but, even your soul, are scary. They require a huge leap of faith just to enter. We know that if this one ends, we will be hurt, and hurt badly. God, I'm a sucker for punishment, 'cause I love those.

Many of us, I know I've done it, will shy away from these encounters. It's human nature; we don't want to feel pain. But it's these relationships, these relationships where we put our heart, mind, and soul on the line, these are the ones worth fighting for.

Oh hell, I'm getting serious. This shit is about to start getting depressing. So let's stop here, let's have a *__"Drink"__*. And let's move on.

"...Kick it in now second wind, we got two more hours to go..."

6 LOVE AND WOMEN

I guess this is where we have landed. The different types of women. This ought to be fun. It will be fun, as well as piss of half of my readers. Having said that, this chapter is mostly directed towards the guys. Though ladies, if you decide to read this chapter, you may learn some things. Or not, but who cares, you already bought the book.

There are two and only two types of women in the world: Good and Bad. That's it; there is no in-between. Period, dot, the end!

If you are with a good woman, stick with her. If you're with a bad one, cut and run dude, or you're gonna be fifty, sitting in an easy chair waiting, praying, hoping to die. If you are with an ok girl, run too, she'll end up being bad. There is no such thing as an "ok" girl. If she seems just alright, there is something you don't know. And believe me, when you figure
it out you're fucked! Thus, she belongs in the bad

category. I may speak often of "ok" girls. Whenever I
do, just put them in the bad category. That's where they
belong, and will eventually end up.

I have been with the "good" ones, the "bad" ones, and
the "ok" ones. Trust me, you do not want the ok ones. The
"good" ones you know they are good. The "bad" ones, well,
at least you know how much life sucks with them. But it's
the "ok" ones that are scary. Unlike the bad ones, you never
know what you are in for. One day everything may be fine,
you're in love, you move in together, the next day she's
hooked on meth and she is trying to
have you killed. (I'll explain that reference later)

How do you tell them apart you ask? Well, let me
open another beer here and I'll tell you. *__"Drink"__* First, a girl
must possess one of two things: either beauty or personality.
You can date a girl who is a complete moron or a complete
bitch as long as she has the looks. The reason being because
then at least you can justify her to your friends, your
family, and yourself. You can say, "Look man, yeah that
wall is smarter, but hey, check out her ass".

Or if she is ugly she must have a great personality.
If your girl is kind, caring, intelligent, and really will
treat you right, that is good. At this point you can over-
look her three hundred pounds, the fact that she has a
horse face, and a hairy lip. The reason being is you can
say, "Yeah man, I know her face scares kids, and yes, she
does smell like stale cheese, but she's really sweet."

Which one is better? Well, neither; both are good.
The best is a girl who has both. A girl who you can tell
your friends, "Dude, she is smart, she treats me nice, and
damn, check out that ass." Those are the characteristics of a
good woman. I know that I just pissed off a whole bunch of
people, but you know what? Fuck you. I'm right.

Same thing goes for you ladies out there. You can
justify one or the other. But having a man with
personality, good looks, and a big dick really helps your
argument.

Now onto the bad. These are the girls who have
neither going for them. These are the girls who are ugly

and bitchy. The ones you describe to your friends as "Yeah, she's a bitch, yeah, she smells funny... damn I'm screwed. Where's my gun?"

If you find yourself with one of these, you don't have to kill yourself, unless you really want to. (Just buy a few copies of my book first so I get the royalties.)

All you have to do is run. Pack your shit, and get the hell out. Stop taking her calls, go somewhere she can't find you, get yourself drunk, and take home someone else. And going home with someone else is actually easier than it seems. Read on and I'll give you the goods, the Holy Grail if you will, on the human female psyche.

Pay very close attention here. I will now describe the scariest of all women: the "ok" ones. These are the girls who are decent looking, who are of average intelligence, and who are relatively nice. These are the ones you describe as all around average. No one is average. It doesn't exist!

These people are hiding something. They will suck you in and when they have their hooks in you, when you pass the point of no return, they spring the trap, and you're fucked. Trust me man, I've been there, watch out for the "ok" ones.

Lou Wise

"Doing crystal meth, will lift you up until you break
It won't stop, I won't come down
I keep stock with the tick-tock rhythm, I bump for the drop
And then I bumped up, I took the hit that I was given
Then I bumped again, then I bumped again…"
-----Third Eye Blind

7 WRONG GIRL

I realize that I have just broken down women into two, possibly three, simple, perhaps offensive categories, but I'm right. Just keep in mind that I am not a psychologist. Some shrink probably could have and should have put it slightly more eloquently, but that does not lessen the validity of my theory. (I love my "Word of the Day" calendar; it has really helped my vocabulary.)

I have, over the course of my (what feels like many) years, I've had relationships with all types of women. Some good (which I fucked up), some bad (which thankfully I fucked up), and some ok (which fucked me up). Allow me, if you will, to share a couple anecdotal stories here.

This story comes from a friend of mine. This story I added because it is the exception to my good, bad, and ok rule. I know what I said, but hey, nothing is absolute, except maybe the fact that the more tattoos and piercings a girl has, the easier she is.

Ok, so where do I start? Let's start with my buddy, we'll call him James. James is a nice guy, fairly good looking, comes from a good family and has a lot of potential. One night as James is stumbling back to his house after a good night of drinking, he sits on a bench outside of his college so he can finish his glass of scotch before heading home. While he's sitting there a girl walks up and sits next to him. Feeling his beer muscles, he decides to start a conversation. Her name ends up being Monnie.

Monnie is a sweet girl, very beautiful, in fact she had done some modeling at one point. Now this girl is out of my boy's league, way out, but being buzzed he tries his best. The conversation goes great. He realizes that she not only is gorgeous, but also quite smart. They end up talking for hours; they seem to like each other. Around four that morning they part and my buddy goes home.

When James arrives at his apartment, all he can think about is Monnie. Unfortunately, he can't remember her phone number. This stupid fuck has just hit it off with the girl of his dreams and has managed to fuck it up. He spends the next hour trying to sober up, trying to remember her number, but he can't. Do you want to know why he can't? He forgot to ask!!! What a tool!!

James is about to start beating his head against the wall again, literally, when he remembers something. He remembered asking about her class schedule. That is when he devised his, depending on who you talk to, very romantic, or very pathetic, plan. James decides that he will wake up early, and be outside of her first class the next morning when she leaves.

He has the idea to "accidentally" bump into her when she leaves class. I didn't think it was the best idea at the time, but you know what? It actually worked. Actually, it took a few days of these "accidental" meetings, but eventually he got a date. That date turned into two. That tuned into meeting the parents, both sets. Next thing you know they've been dating for two years.

Now, it's two years later, James has got the best of everything in a girl. She's smart, pretty, kind, and I believe they love each other. And this is when they decided to move in together. Moving in with a chick is a huge step, but I'll get into that later.

They find a very nice, very yuppyish apartment, sign the papers, discuss it with the parents, and go for it. James moves his stuff in while Monnie is out of town working at a summer job that her folks got for her. When she finally moves in, it lasts about three days. No, they didn't get on each other's nerves; they weren't fighting because they now had to share a flat. So why did they only last three days?

Well, since I have wasted a few pages on this story already, I'm gonna make the explanation real short, real sweet. The simple version is that while at her summer job she met this thirty-plus year old felon, who was recently paroled, who got her addicted to Crystal Meth, and with who she devised a plan to kill James. No shit, it's all true.

Don't worry, James is fine. Thankfully, he is a sneaky fuck who figured out what was going on and was able to avoid the planned unpleasantness.

Why did I tell you this story? Well, mainly because I wanted you to be on guard, always. Even though Monnie wasn't a typical "ok" girl, at the top of the scale, she still went nuts. It can happen, just think about the possibilities if she hadn't been in the good category. What would have happened if she were in the "ok" category from the start? Think about how really fucked up this story might have been. It may have ended with James being ground up, and becoming the secret ingredient in a really tasty Bloody Mary. ***"Drink"***

Here, I promise this is the last story on relationships. I add this one for personal reasons. There are times in life when even the best relationships are hopeless. It may not be the fault of anyone involved, it's just that the timing was wrong. This sums up the following story.

I was in a BAD relationship. When I say bad, you have no idea what bad means. I'll save that story for the next book, it would fill the entire fucking thing. But as I was exiting the horrible, absolutely soul crushing relationship that I was in, I found THE GIRL. "THE GIRL'S" name was Presaria.

Presaria was amazing. Her skin was pale, almost translucent, her hair autumn red. She was slender, with perfect smallish breasts, which were always under simple t-shirts. She was extravagantly beautiful.

We had flirted for a while, kissed, it was great. Then one night I needed her, not sexually, I just needed her. I was in a bind, I needed someone I could trust, someone I could turn to, confide in, and when I called her, she came. It was wonderful.

From that point on we were inseparable. We sat, we talked, we actually had a relationship that spanned the simple physical attraction. (Don't get me wrong, I wanted her more than you know, and "*it*" was great. The attraction went beyond all that.)

It went this way for a few months. And believe me, it shouldn't have lasted as long as it did. There was tons of stress put on our relationship. My ex was always showing up, calling, trying to screw us up. So was her ex. I did something that went above and beyond the criteria for getting dumped. (No I won't tell you what it was.) But we persisted through it all.

Then one day it ended. Don't ask me exactly why, I'm not totally sure, though I have my suspicions. One day I get a call, Presaria is stopping by the house. When she shows up she sits on my couch, lights a cigarette, and says I can't see you anymore, I can't be your girlfriend. And that was that. Talk about an anticlimactic fucking break-up.

Why did I tell that story? Fuck if I know. Maybe I hope she reads it… maybe I want to warn all of you not to take for granted what you have. Perhaps if I treated her with more respect, perhaps if I were a better man, perhaps she would have stayed. Who knows, take from that story what you will.

After writing all these stories, you know what? Fuck relationships! *__"Drink"__* That's right, fuck relationships! *__"Drink"__*

Relationships, they are the greatest and the worst things on the planet. The more you love, the more it may hurt you. My rules, consider them guidelines. There are no real rules, I'm full of shit. The truth, the absolute truth is this: if you engage in a relationship, you will get hurt. If you don't, you are one of the fortunate few, one of the lucky ones. DO NOT FUCK IT UP!! I will hunt you down!

"...I treat my body like a temple, you treat yours like a tent..."

----- Jimmy Buffett

8 BODY TYPES

If categorizing women into simple categories pissed some of you off, this next chapter will really put you over the edge. Before I begin, I need to apologize to my publisher. You are gonna get *so* many letters about this chapter. Most of which I can guess are going to be unpleasant.

There are certain stereotypes that people fit into just because of the way they look. These stereotypes do not just fit women, I will piss off guys at the same time. I am an equal opportunity offender. I don't play favorites. But, just in case you are the type of person who gets easily offended...
"Drink!"

Fat Chicks: Fat chicks know that they are fat. They know that there may be fifty or sixty other girls in the bar who are better looking, who lack the tonnage. But unfortunately, the fat chicks want attention, they want a man too. So what do they do? They don't have the looks; they know that. They know that if they have a good personality no one will notice it in a loud club. So what's left? They have to be easy; they have to put out.

Wait, before you kill me, I am right! Think about it. Go to a bar, go to a club, look at the fat chicks. They are dressed like fat whores. They have the daisy duke shorts showing off their ass rolls, the tube tops where their fat gut hangs out, the tattoos on their big ass cleavage. Yes, it's gross, but it sends a message that says, "You may not want this, but I'm offering and you're drunk."

Fuck you, I hear you. But I'm right. Think about it. What else does a fat chick have to offer?

Guys with towels: We have all seen this guy at a bar. He's the big guy who has a towel wrapped around his neck. What the fuck is that about. It looks fucking stupid. Who the hell stands there in front of the mirror going, "Nice shoes...check, jeans...check, cool shirt...check, hundred dollar chain... check, thousand dollar watch... check. Wait, what am I missing? Oh yeah, a fucking towel around my neck."

You might as well hang a sign around your neck saying that you are a fat, sweaty pig. When you have to plan ahead to bring a sweat rag out with you, you have a gland problem, see a doctor. Please! Anything, just leave the towel at home.

Girls, I beg you, let these guys know that they look stupid. How can you find a guy with a sweat rag around his neck attractive? Yea, in the gym when he's working out, maybe. But at a bar? Damn! It's gross.

Tattooed ladies: How do I say this...is there an easy way, a polite, intelligent way of expressing my next thought? Probably, but I don't care. The more piercings or tattoos a girl has, the easier she is.

Why is this you ask? Well, I have my own theory, it may be right, it may be wrong, but either way I'm still right. The more tattoos she has, the quicker you'll get her in bed.

Here's my theory. A person gets tattoos to show them off, the more tattoos a person has the more they want to show. Thus, a girl with a ton of tats will show you more of her body.

Why else would a girl get a tattoo on her inner-pelvic region or on her breasts? She wants to show you that part of her body. She wants you to look, to fantasize, and to take notice. It's the same reason that girls get their nipples pierced, they want you to look, they want to show you. How about tongue piercings? As far as I know there is one, and only one, reason for getting your tongue pierced. If you don't know what that is, you are way too young to be reading this book.

Trust me guys, if you want a sure thing, go into the bar and find the chick with the most piercings and tattoos. Girls, if you want to be a sure thing, go out, get a bunch of tats, and show them off. I guarantee guys will flock to you.

"...I go for younger women, lived with several awhile..."
-----Jimmy Buffett

9 LIVING TOGETHER

As I said in the last chapter, at least I think it was the last chapter, well maybe the chapter before, I don't know, I've been drinking a lot. Join me ***"Drink"***
Moving in together is a HUGE jump. Let me repeat myself here for effect: IT IS HUGE!! Most of you know this already. You know that you have to split bills, which by the way guys means you will end up paying for everything. You know that you will be spending just about every waking moment together. But there are a lot of things that you don't know. Let me, a man who has lived with a few different girls, school you.

Also, if there are any girls I have not completely offended yet and who are still reading along, the following words of advice were also gathered from speaking with many of my female friends.

Let me start by saying that I am not against two people moving in together. In fact, I think if you can live with someone, you are one step closer to the dreaded "M" word, and God bless you for it. I'm just informing those among you who may be unsure of their decision, of what they are in for.

First, let's talk about privacy. What can I say about privacy? Except that there is none! Kiss it goodbye buddy.

The day you move in with someone, you should take any expectation of privacy and toss it out the fucking window. Seriously man, it's gone. You wake up, your partner is there. You come home from work, still there. You have a tough day on the job, you come home and just want to sit in front of the T.V. and have a beer? Well then I hope you don't mind watching the tube, drinking your beer, and rubbing her feet all at the same time. ***"Drink"***

Guys and gals, we all have those days when we just need to be alone. Just need to sit and play video games or drink or talk with a long lost friend on the phone, or look at porn on the Internet or whatever. Those days are gone. See-ya, adios, fucking gone. Peace out, no more.

As soon as you live together, you are accountable to someone else. You want to buy something, you have to justify it. You can no longer work late without feeling guilty, having to apologize, or negotiate. Your time is under new management.

I know many of you can get past the whole privacy issue. I hear you out there, "I want to spend my life with this person… we will share everything". Yeah, yeah, blah blah. Just wait, you obviously have no idea what sharing everything means, dumb-ass.

We all have those little things that we do to make ourselves more attractive to the opposite sex. The opposite sex does many things that make them more attractive to us. Let me tell you, it is a huge turn off when you see them do these little things.

For example, most guys like girls who are not hairy. Let me set a scene for you. You and your girl are in the shower, you're soaping each other up, the water's warm, your touching here and touching there, maybe you get a piece. Then suddenly she reaches for her razor and begins to shave her pits. It may not sound like much but damn, it's a huge turn off. You think that's bad, just wait till the day comes that she decides to change her tampon in front of you…talk about fucked up.

Shit guys, the girls will agree with me on this one. From my experience, and that of girls who I have talked to, nobody likes watching a girl, nor do girls like having someone watch this. It takes the whole allure out of the process. C'mon no one wants to think of his or her girl as hairy beasts. Guess what? They are hairy; it's fucking nature. But, it's just one of those things that girls do, they de-hair themselves, we don't need to think about. But when you live together, you will know about it. You will know everything…things you really, really do not want to know.

How many of you like reading while you take a nice long dump? I do, and I'm guessing a vast majority of you do too. Well guess what? Those days are over. That is, unless you like your girl popping her head in, trying to hurry you up, or just coming in to brush her teeth while you're on the pot.

And guys, you know that there are times when you really don't want to be disturbed. Perhaps, you're like me, and have tried to realize that once you move in with a girl this is your stronghold, this is your throne, this is where you retreat to be alone. You should also realize that there are times when you have been drinking, when you and your buddies thought it was a good idea to hit the all night taco joint, that you think it unconstitutional for anyone to enter the bathroom because it would constitute cruel and unusual punishment. But guess what? Those are the nights when your girl will enter. How embarrassing!

To add to that, girls take huge, nasty, smelly, shits too. I know, it is a common misconception among us guys, but yes, girls do shit too. That third hole is not just a really tight place to… well you get the idea. Just wait till you walk in one day and your girl has just taken a huge dump. The kind that would gag a maggot. How sexy will you find her later. It will definitely make you think twice before taking her to a Mexican restaurant again. A "Dirty Sanchez" takes on a whole new fucking meaning. Believe you me.

If you can get past these things, good, great. It really helps if you are head over heels in love with her first. These things can really fuck up a relationship if you are not prepared.

Lou Wise

"...I Never Got Over Those Blue Eyes, I See Them Every Where, I Miss The Arms That Held Me, When All Of The Love Was There...There's Someone For Me Somewhere....And I Still Miss Someone"

----- Johnny Cash

10 I THINK I AM IN LOVE

Having said all that, let me clarify a few things. I am in love. I have been for nearly seven years now. So why do I rant and rave about love, women and why I should have been a priest? Well, that's simple: because loves fucks with you. It is perhaps the one emotion that has the ability to truly screw with one's head. Now having said *that*, let me tell you a story.

Returning from college one summer, I was hanging around with my girlfriend Cathy and she decided to introduce me to her friends. Now this was good and bad. Good for me, bad for her.

Good for me because her friends were more fun than she was, so at least now I could enjoy myself when we hung out; bad for her because this is where I met Krystal. (Yes I know I spelled it wrong, purposefully though. For those of you who know me, you'll get the reference. For those of you who don't get it, that's the point.)

Now Krystal is not what I thought my ideal girl was going to be. She is not the type of girl to turn every head when she walks into the room, most, but not all. She was politically so far to the other side than I that it was comical.

We spent the next few years flirting. I know it sounds sad but that's what we did. I would come home, run into the old crew, and hang out with Krystal. We would go out, go to the bars, play pool, find excuses to sit next to each other, touch each other, ect, ect. It really was pathetic.

So why didn't we ever hook up? Well, usually one of us had a

37

significant other, or in my case a less than significant other. She had morals, I didn't care, I had been putting the moves on her for years. A monogamous relationship was not going to stand in my way. I know what you're thinking, there is no way in all those years that the opportunity didn't arise. Well, it did a few times but I usually screwed it up.

One night we were hanging out, probably during year two of our pathetic flirting, just sitting in my car outside of her house drinking a few beers and talking. Now I want nothing more than to just lean over, kiss this girl and live happily ever after, well at least live happily for the next twenty or thirty minutes. (I'm being sarcastic, ladies I can go forever. And by forever I mean 5 minutes tops.) But I don't. I'm scared. I am so afraid that it's the beer talking, and that as soon as I lean in for the kiss, she's gonna pull away, end the conversation and from that point on things would be weird. I was so afraid of screwing up this friendship that I was willing to let the opportunity pass.

I know if there is a woman who I have not yet offended by this point and is still reading this rag, she's probably thinking how sweet. How thoughtful, how kind, how romantic it is that this man would forsake pleasures of the flesh in order to keep a friend. Many of these women are thinking that I did the right thing. Bullshit! I wasn't thinking any of those things.

I didn't do the right thing. I fucked up. Why? Let me tell you why. After sitting in the car talking all night, it was time for Krystal to leave. As she slowly moved her slender body out of the car, I still wanted to pull her close and kiss her. As she shut the door, she stuck her head back in the window and asked, "Why didn't you kiss me tonight?"

"Why didn't you kiss me tonight!!" "Why didn't you kiss me tonight!!!!" Son of a bitch! Why didn't I kiss her! I had no idea what to say. How do you answer that question? For once I decided to be honest. I told her, "I was scared, I wasn't sure if you wanted to or not. I didn't want to screw up this friendship."

"Screw up this friendship?" she replied, "I've been sitting here all night with you hoping, waiting for you to make a move. But now I guess the moment has passed. It's late and it would be awkward if we did anything now. Goodnight Lou." (I am such a fucking loser.)

Talk about a kick in the ass. I had been agonizing over should I or shouldn't I, what would she think if I did. Well apparently we know now what she would think.

Take this piece of advice: don't hesitate, don't pause, go with your instincts. Who knows what would have happened if I would have made that move. The possibilities are endless.

The part that sucks the most is that I know what did happen. We have spent the next four or five years waiting for opportunities to arise.

Just so as not to have my boys think that I am a complete tool, we have "hooked up" over the years. And yes, it was incredible. Hell, when we "hooked up," I was probably the happiest man on the planet. The only person happier is some third world country farmer who has just been given a second goat.

Plus, it was more than just polite intercourse, I realized how much I loved this girl and have spent the past few years trying to win her. Unfortunately my pursuits have been less than successful. I'm not saying that we couldn't just hook up, we have (wink, wink), but I want more. I want to be the guy with the second goat. I want to close the geographical divide between us. I know that we may not live happily ever after, hell we may only last a week, but I still want to try. I don't want to grow old thinking what if. Life should never contain what ifs. (Shit, the goat could die after a week.)

If you can sit back and say what if to anything, you have a problem. Now go fix it. What's the worst that can happen? The way I see it there are two possibilities to every what if. The first is it works out. You can sit back and say, "Hell yeah, that was cool. I'm glad I did it." Or, it'll suck. Then you sit there, you say, "That was dumb," and you move the fuck on. Big deal, no one hurt, at least not that much. And you can always go back and fix things. You can't go back and fix a missed opportunity. It will never be fixed. You had the chance, you blew it. Don't live with it. Don't put yourself in that position.

Here is another example. This story may sound quite similar to the last. Guess what it is? It's not here because I am not creative enough to think up something new, something different. It is a reoccurring pattern in my life. Read the story and I'll explain.

Alright, this next story may not fit. I don't know where this story is going. All I know is that while writing this book, I stumbled upon a really weird situation. Let me start by saying I believed that I have had it all figured out. I know women, I know how relationships, how the "game" works. But then all of a sudden your entire view gets fucked up. Something happens and, well shit, all your theories, all your prior knowledge goes out the window. This next story is one of those exceptions to the rule.

Let me start by saying when I "met" this girl, it was purely sexual. This girl is cute, fuck that, she is hot. Plus she has this raw sexuality about her that drives men

insane. This is how we met. We both found each other very attractive, we "hooked up." We have talked about our sexual interests, about what we want sexually, and we have acted on a few of those fantasies.

Hell yeah. What more could you want, a girl who is open to just about anything? Now that is cool. So why am I telling you this? Is it just to rub your face in

it? No. I will relate this story to you simply to point out that relationships are very, *Very*, complex.

Here, I have this girl she is hot, she is very open sexually, and yet I have a problem. "Impossible," you say. But no it is true. The first few times I hung out with this girl I had one thing on my mind. Take a wild guess what that was.

One night I call her and she agrees to come over. I'm thinking, "Hell yeah, I'm gonna get some." She shows up, looking quite cute, I offer her a drink, and we begin to talk. Next thing I know it's five hours later, we're still drinking, and we are talking. It's been five damn hours and I haven't made a move. I have been enjoying the conversation so much that I forgot about sex. This was not a what if situation, I truly forgot about sex. I have no idea how that ever fucking happened.

I cannot believe that I have sat here for so long, talking, drinking, with a member of the opposite sex and have not tried to sleep with them. I must be slipping. What, you ask could make me forget about hooking up? I'll tell you, she is smart.

Saying that she is smart is an understatement. This girl is brilliant. We sat there for hours discussing literature. We talked about Fitzgerald, King, Meltzer, Ludlum, Karowack, Patterson, and a multitude of others.

For some reason this conversation made me forget my primal instincts.

So we had a good night. No, we had a great night. It was an enigma. It was something out of the ordinary. Next time things would be different. I would be back to my old, shameless self.

Guess what? They weren't. I had invited her over again, I was determined, at least I thought I was, to "fix this problem". I was going to enjoy *all* the aspects of her company. I was going to talk with her, which was one thing that I did enjoy, and have some carnal fun. Well, at least that was what I thought I was going to do.

I didn't, it was so much more. How can that be? Let me explain, I enjoyed her company. I really enjoyed her company. You want to know how far I got don't you? Well, you're in luck, I'm gonna tell you. I hope you can handle this. It may get a little freaky. ***"Drink"***

I kissed her. That's right, all I did was kiss her. And it was amazing. What? A kiss? All that build up for a simple kiss? I hear you yelling, asking all of those questions, and I will explain. True, part of me was hoping to "get some", I won't lie. But the majority of me wanted to just talk to her.

Sounds strange right? It isn't. It was as close to perfection as I have ever been. Being able to sit with someone whom you find extremely attractive, someone who you find very sexually appealing, and find yourself wanting nothing more than to sit and talk. Find yourself hanging on every word, just waiting, wanting to hear what was to come out of her next. That is beautiful.

So where does that leave me now? Well, I don't know. I go to visit her most nights at work. When she gets a chance she may sit and talk for a bit, sometimes not. But either way, I love it watching her. Waiting till she sneaks me a look, a smile, words do not do it justice.

Oh man, check this out. The other night I was at the bar where she worked and she went up on stage to sing. Now I have heard her sing before, and she is good. This night, holy shit, she was amazing. I was mesmerized. I just sat there listening to her low, rich voice serenade the crowd. I was entranced. And that's it. I fell for her that night. Looking into her eyes, it was as if she was singing only to me. Unfortunately, that's where the story ends. Perhaps in volume two I may have an update.

The reoccurring theme that I mentioned, it should be obvious by now. If not I'll spell it out for you. I hesitate. I ask what ifs. That is bad. I hate what ifs. I know what I should do, what I want to do. But for some reason I don't. I promise you, my readers, my audience, that I will no longer fall into the what if trap. I will break free!

For example, my first test. As I sit here I am slowly drinking a Coors Original, but on the other side of the desk is a bottle of shitty tequila. What if instead of slowly enjoying this beer I reach across my desk grab the bottle of tequila, and take a huge chug off of it?

Well as I said before there should be no what ifs, so here we go. Let's put down this frosty cold beer, reach across past the computer, past the stapler, and wrap my hands around the 1.75 liter bottle of Mexico's worst tequila. As I pull the bottle close I begin thinking of all the problems that this could cause. I could get sick, I could get drunk, I could rip my clothes off and go chase the neighbor's cat (even though I promised them I wouldn't do that again). But no what ifs!

I sit here and stare at this bottle. I slowly feel my hand rise to the cap and begin to unscrew it. Now there is nothing between me and the booze except a little air. Just like what was between me and Krystal's lips, only air. Fuck it! I'm going for it!

GODDAMN THAT BURNS!!! Whoa I feel good! See? No what ifs. Let's see what happens next. ***"Drink"***

Lou Wise

"Love the kind you clean up with a mop and bucket
Like the lost catacombs of Egypt only God knows where we stuck it"
----- Blood Hound Gang

11 SEX

Oh shit here we go! I'm drunk, the juices are flowing, and now we get to the fun stuff. This ought to get real interesting. "***Drink***" Just to make sure we are all on the same page, I want you to catch up. "***Drink***" Have I made myself perfectly clear? "***Drink***" I need you all in the same mindset here, it would make me feel a whole lot more comfortable. "***Drink!***"

First, a public service message about sex: guys, don't be a fool, wrap your tool. There are so many reasons for this, so listen carefully. You too girls, make your man put on his jimmy hat. No one wants a burning sensation when they pee. And that's one of the best things that can happen. How about kids? Was that one night fling worth having to raise a child? Having a child will screw up your life as well as the kid's if you're not ready for one. Or worse, AIDS. Do you really want to die because you wanted to bust a nut? I don't think so.

I know, you think it won't happen to you. It happens to someone else. Bullshit! You are that someone else. Just wait till you're popping pills and drinking cranberry juice. Or, you spend days in agony while your girl takes pregnancy tests. It is not cool. Trust me. Been there, done that.

Yeah, yeah, blah, blah, it feels better without one. I know you want the flesh on flesh feel. It is not worth the risk man. Strap one on, go to town, let her get hers, and then there are plenty of other ways to get off without that flesh on flesh feel.

I know some of you may think that is not as much fun. Guess what? You suck then. People who say that are the "girl lays down, guy get on top, pounds away, and it ends" type of people. Sex like that sucks whether you're wearing your raincoat or not. That type of sex is not fun. I mean it is, but it can be much better. Move around a bit, try new things, new positions, new places, ect, ect.

But I'll pull out you say. Yeah, trust me, that doesn't work all the time. But, if you really want to do the pull out method, do it this way: get in there, pound away, pull out, then take off the condom, and get off some other way. That's the pull out method that truly works.

Follow my advice, please. Sex can be **a** beautiful thing, or it can be a dirty self-serving thing. And both can be kinda cool. But either way, be fucking smart about it, be creative. Buy a book on it, rent a movie, learn some new moves. Enough of the public service message. On with the story.

I am about to bear my soul, my own views, and perversions regarding sex, as well as those of my friends. They are going to kill me when this book is published. Shit, I have even stolen stories that friends have told about other friends. I am about to make a whole bunch of enemies. You bastards out there better appreciate this. I'm gonna get beat within an inch of my life for you so you better be damn grateful!

Sex is fun. I love sex! Let me say again I LOVE SEX!! Sex, as I see it, is like pizza, even when it's bad its good. But, sex isn't all that it is cracked up to be.

That should cover the moral, or immoral, view of sex depending on your beliefs. Now, here are a bunch of stories that are funny as hell and may well have some advice hidden in them. Probably not, but I'll try to find one so my publisher doesn't cut them.

I know this guy, well actually I don't know him, I heard this story from a friend but it is damn good. There is this guy, we'll call him Joe. Joe, is a nice guy, a little full of himself but a nice guy. Unfortunately Joe hasn't been laid in nearly two years. (This may account for why he is a prick at times.) This is the story of how Joe didn't break his losing streak, and probably why he hasn't been laid in two years.

One night Joe and his buddy are at a small little bar, kind of seedy, but a nice place none the less. They are about to leave when Joe's buddy runs into two girls that he knows. Joe and the buddy invite the girls over to join them, and they do. Now Joe's buddy is trying to be a good wing man, so he throws himself under the bus trying to make Joe look good. It works.

Joe ends up leaving with one of the girls. This girl, Maurina, invites Joe back to her house. Joe, slightly buzzed, accepts. So Joe and Maurina are back at her place, they sit, talk and go through a few bottles of wine. Things are looking really good for Joe.

At one point, after a few hours and a few bottles, Joe and Maurina go to the kitchen to "pour another drink". Bullshit, Maurina wants some cock. Once there, Maurina hops up on the counter and waits for Joe to open another bottle, once he pours the drinks, Maurina pulls him close, pulls him right between her now spread legs and kisses him. Joe, being a man of quite considerable size, picks Maurina up and carries her to the bedroom. Joe scores, right? Nope. Not Joe. He does the dumbest thing I have ever heard of a man doing.

He carries her to the bedroom and passionately throws her onto the bed. She lands on her back and tears her shirt off. Her bare skin looks amazing against the purple satin sheets. Joe undoes the top button of his shirt and takes a step back. She expects him to rip her clothes off, or his clothes. Does Joe do this? Nope. Joe, taking a step back, places his hands on his hips (imagine a Superman-esque pose) and says, " I Will Not Have Sex With You!"

What the fuck? What the fuck is that! This asshole hasn't been laid in two fucking years. Here he has a girl, who is willing, able, and God knows wants to screw his brain out, and he says, "I Will Not Have Sex With You!" What the fuck was he thinking?

Needless to say, Maurina did not take this very well. Not only does she feel rejected, but she is flabbergasted. The situation deteriorates from here. Now thoroughly pissed, Maurina takes the offensive. She says, " Just because you have me in my room doesn't mean I was gonna fuck you. Where do you get off thinking that I was?"

Now we all know that Maurina wanted to sleep with Joe. It was his presumptions that killed the deal. Yes, yes, I hear you. Some of you say it is good, moral even, that he didn't sleep with her that night. You may be right. But he could have been a bit more suave about it. He didn't have to pretend he was a superhero when he shot her down. Oh, and wait, he hadn't been laid in two years!!! He shouldn't be telling anyone no.

Plus, it's not like he got some eighteen-year-old freshman drunk and took advantage of her. This was a mature woman, someone who knows the game. She knew what she wanted. He should have gone for the gold. I know that may make me sound shallow, and I am, but it's true.

Here's the moral of that story. First, if you haven't been laid in that long, and you bitch about it all the time, don't turn anyone down. Second, even if you think that it is wrong to sleep with someone on the first date, even when they want to, let them know it politely. Please, I beg you be slightly more eloquent than this guy Joe. You'll thank me for it.

Oh God, this one is good. There is this guy, we'll call him Rick. Rick is another nice guy, kinda shy, your average good guy. Rick is dating this chick named Amy. Amy is younger, but legal, and is very cute. Rick and Amy have a very good, very healthy sex life. Amy has only two complaints, not really complaints, more like requests. The first is that she wants Rick to masturbate in front of her. More specifically, she wants to strip her clothes off and watch Rick jerk-off while watching her. Here lies a few problems.

One, guys, back me up on this, there are a lot of reasons why Rick doesn't and should not do this. First, when guys jerk off while they're in a committed relationship, they are not thinking about their girlfriend. If they wanted to get off while thinking about their girlfriend, they would have sex with her.

Second, when guys jack–off, it is not sexy. It's this awkward rubbing motion. Followed by a grunt and a mess. This is not something that anyone should find sexy. Plus, why would you jerk off in front of someone? If they are naked, and you have your piece in your hand, why not just insert it somewhere, or let them do the stroking? I never understood the whole "mutual masturbation craze."

The second request she had was that Rick be "louder" during sex. "Being louder" was an understatement. Rick, being a shy guy, was quiet. The dead made more noise than him in bed. Amy wanted him to simply make more noise in bed.

Rick and Amy actually talked, discussed, and argued about this. Finally, they compromised. They agreed that as a start, Rick would at least say something, anything as he came.

So here they are, in Amy's bed, Rick's on top pounding away and thinking. Rick in fact is freaking out. He has no idea what to say. Thousands of different things are running through his head. He could say "yes," or "I'm gonna come," or "oh baby," or "Amy," or any number of things. Finally, just as he is about to finish, he decides what he will say.

This is fucking priceless! As Rick finishes, he says, no he yells, "SHA--- ZAAAM!". I'm talking full on, accent and all, Gomer Pile from *F-Troop*, sha-zaam. What the fuck! That was the wrong thing to say.

Talking to Rick, he has told me that at the time, in his head, "Sha—zaam" sounded like a good idea. You know what? If it sounded like a good idea in his head that is where it should have stayed. But I bet you don't care about this; you want to know what Amy did.

Well, as soon as Rick yells the infamous "Sha—zaam" everything stops. I mean dead stop, no more trusts, no more movement. They just lay there and stare at each other. After a few awkward moments, Amy says, "Get off me."

Rick complies and now they are laying there next to each other. After a several very tense minutes, Amy Finally speaks. "Don't do that again…ever." Needless to say Rick never does. Well, that's not entirely true. Since Rick and Amy have split, Rick has found that whenever he wants to piss a girl off, to end the relationship he is in, he pulls the old "Sha—zaam" line. You know what? It works every time. ***"Drink"***

Here's a story that is nearly unbelievable. Not that the moronic actions of the tools in the last few stories are any more believable. This is the story of a ballsy, perhaps distorted mind. A story that many of us mere mortals would like to accomplish, but simply can't even try. Let me explain.

Two guys go out to a bar, Matt and Mike. Matt and Mike are the best of friends, they have known each other for years, but are quite different. Mike is reserved and quiet; while Matt is loud, confident, and has no fear (especially after a few shots of Jack).

While Mike and Matt are sitting at the bar getting completely obliterated, Mike doing shots of tequila, Matt drinking his Jack, when two girls walk in. L u c k i l y , Mike knows the two girls, and invites them to join him and Matt. This is when the real drinking starts.

After a few rounds, it is obvious which girl is hooking up with which guy. After a few more rounds just to "seal the deal," they all decide to leave. They drive down a deserted, dead end street and park. Mike is in one car with his chick, Matt is in the other with his. Mike, being shy, and not being too interested in the girl he has with him, slowly and eloquently, shuts the girl down. (He is not as big of a tool as Joe.)

The blow off is ok with Mike's girl. Even though she wants him, she is more interested in what her friend is doing. She loves gossip. Mike and his chick decide to leave their car, and sneak up on Matt and his girl. Slowly Mike and the girl exit the car, and sneak up beside Matt's.

Mike has lucked out. His timing couldn't have been any better. He arrives just in time to hear one of the best, most arrogant, successful lines ever delivered by a man. When Mike arrives, he peeks in the car, and see's Matt and the girl kissing. Suddenly, they stop, and Matt pulls away. Fearing he has been spotted, Mike drops out of sight and listens. This is what Mike hears:

" So, are you gonna blow me or what?"

Mike at this point is holding his breath, waiting to hear the girl slap Matt and jump out of the car. For some reason, all Mike hears is silence. Mike is confused. Mike risks a glance into the car. What he sees is… the girl going to town on Matt's, well, you know.

Mike couldn't believe it, and neither can I. Any other man who would brazenly ask some chick that he just met in a bar to blow him would and should get slapped. But not Matt. There is something about him. Matt my friend, my hat's off to you.

I cannot believe that I have just told you all of these stories. These are embarrassing stories about myself and embarrassing stories that my friends have told me in the strictest of confidences. I swore I would never tell anyone. Oops. So you guys have to swear not to tell anyone either. Ok?

In fact, I think after you read this chapter, rip the pages out and mail them back to the publisher. Maybe my friends won't catch on.

Lou Wise

"Can't you see I'm easily bothered by persistence
One step from lashing out at you..."
----- Pantera

12 FUCK THE MALL

As you can probably tell by the title of this chapter, I am not a big fan of malls. I have been to malls in New York, Florida, California, Georgia, half a dozen other states, and even that big ass one in Minnesota. And you know what I have learned after visiting all of these malls? They fucking suck. Every last one of them.

If I sound bitter, you're right, I am. I firmly believe that malls will be the downfall of American society. I hear you out there, or maybe it's just my neighbor telling me to turn the radio down. "Hey fuck you! Margarittaville kicks ass!" Oh shit, where was I? Oh right, I know that you're thinking I'm overreacting about malls being the downfall of American society... Well, I'm not.

Hear me out. Think about the last time you went to a mall. Were you happy to be there? Can you remember anyone being happy about being at the mall? No, you can't. If you think you can, you're wrong. Don't believe me? Go to the mall, waste a few hours
of your life, and look around. Nobody's happy.

For those of you who have better things to do than waste precious moments of your life going to the mall, let me describe for you a typical trip. First, I have to get in my car and drive the twenty or so minutes to the mall. All along this drive I see plenty of stores where I could buy the shit I need, but *no*, I am going to the mall. So after I waste time and gas, fighting traffic, I pull into the parking lot.

All I see for fucking miles is filled parking spots. So now I have to begin the time honored tradition of all mall patrons: the act of driving up

49

and down the rows hoping and praying that a spot opens up. One never does. You always end up parking two and a half miles from the damn entrance. And it's usually nowhere near the entrance that you wanted to go into in the first place.

I have just wasted forty-five minutes of my life driving to the mall, looking for a parking space, then walking across the damn lot. I will never get this time back. I hope you appreciate this.

Well, I'm in the mall now, and the first people I see are the security guards. Boy, don't these fine high school drop-outs look happy. I know I feel safer knowing Gomer here is on duty.

At this point I'm tired from my little (And by little I mean little as in Herpes is a *little* annoying) trek across the parking lot and I need a place to sit, relax, and thank God that I graduated the eighth grade. Wouldn't want to end up as a security guard. So I search for a place to sit. The only place to sit that I can see is at a table outside a little coffee shop. But of course only customers can sit there, so I have to buy something.

I walk into the way too trendy coffee bar, stroll up to the counter and wait for someone to help me. After waiting way too long at the counter this pink haired, ring through the nose, eighteen year old waste of life walks up and asks me what I want. Here's how the conversation goes:

"What do you want?" asks the waste.

"Isn't this a coffee bar?" I reply

"Yeah."

"Then I'll have a scotch."

"We don't have that, man. We only serve coffee," responds the waste. "Then why the fuck did you ask what I wanted?" I politely reply.

"Well, um, uh, what flavor coffee do you want?" the waste asks.

"What flavor...let me see, what flavor coffee would I like? Call me crazy but I

think I'm gonna try your coffee flavored coffee."

"Coffee flavored?" the now really confused waste asks. "I don't think we have that flavor"

"Let me get this straight. This is a coffee bar, and you don't sell coffee that tastes like fucking coffee?" I want to kill him.

"Yeah."

" Well perhaps do you have anything that closely resembles coffee flavored coffee? I ask.

"We have this house blend, it's a mix of…of, wait, let me find out."

"No! Fine, I'll take the damn house blend shit. Fuck, whatever just give me the damn coffee!" I'm really trying not to kill the kid.

"What size?" he asks

"Large."

"We don't have large, we have…"

"Stop!" This kid is so fucking dead. "I see three cups here on your counter. One is smaller than the other two, one is in the middle, and one is bigger, perhaps one might say larger than the rest. Give me that one. I don't give a shit what trendy name you have for it, I want the big fucking cup!"

"Ok." So the waste walks off and begins to pour. "What do you want in your coffee?"

"Some hot water and beans."

"I don't get it? Do you want milk, cream…."

"Just put it in the fucking cup."

"Alright, that'll be seven bucks."

At this point, if I had not just paid seven bucks for the most stressful coffee buying experience of my life I would have shoved this cup so far up that kid's ass… but now I really need to sit. I'm about to have a damn heart attack. So I go out to the table and sit. *__"Drink!"__*

It is here that I begin my people watching. Trust me it is very easy to spot the unhappy people in the mall. For starters, the waste who sold me this seven dollar cup of shitty coffee was not happy. And after our little incident, he's definitely not happy and now confused.

Speaking of mall employees, let me look around at the other fine merchants in this Mecca of commerce. Just what I thought; they're all miserable. They don't want to be here. They don't want to have to sell you useless crap at way too high prices. Don't get me wrong, I'm not trying to imply that mall employees have a conscience, quite the contrary, I just think they don't want to deal with you.

Think about it. Most mall employees are these young high school and college kids who need a job. They are forced to take jobs that nobody else wants. Which would explain why they work in a mall. (Let's have a ***"Drink"*** for them")

The next group of people that I witness are the ever present teens who you will find in every mall in the world. Why do you think it is that teens are always hanging out at the mall? I'll tell you, it's because there is nothing else for teens to do. They can't go to the bar, most can't drive, and their parents are probably at home so they can't hang there. What else is there for a kid to do?

It's for this reason that I think these kids are unhappily congregating at the mall. They realize that their lives are boring and that this is their only option. Man, that's gotta suck. I think I'll finish my beer as a salute to all those bored teens with limited options. "***Drink.***" Kids, don't lose hope. In a few years you'll be in a bar, drunk, and either puking on yourself or going home with someone a bit too ugly.

Now, which group of unhappy bastards is next? Oh, right, the adults. I'll break this group down into two categories: Parents and Soulless Suckers. First, let's discuss the parents.

Most parents don't want to be at the mall if their sole purpose for being there is to follow their hormone filled teens around while the aforementioned teens try to flirt, or attempt to have their parents buy them useless crap. You know what I'm talking about.

These are the people walking behind a group of adolescents who either drag them into every store looking for the right pair of jeans or the right shirt. Yea they look real happy. These are also the ones who must keep constant vigil so as not to lose their kids behind some shop display where they will try and make out with their new "friend".

Then there are what I call the soulless suckers. These are the people who, for lack of a better word, whore at the mall and will try to sell you tons of useless overpriced shit.

The one who sell you light up antennas for your cell phone, crappy hemp jewelry, BOGO ear piercings, forty dollar hats, and the worst of all those who try and sell you sunglasses. I had a run in with one of these sunglass selling Soulless Suckers on this particular trip.

Here's how this conversation went:
"May I help you, sir?" asked Kiosk boy.
'Yes, thank you. How much are these sunglasses?"
"Two-hundred and nineteen dollars. Can I wrap them up for you or would you like to wear them out?"
"How do you live with yourself you prick?" I ask Kiosk boy very politely.

Needless to say, the conversation deteriorated from there and I was forced to cut my very exciting, enjoyable, and intellectually stimulating trip to the mall short.

Lou Wise

Book Two: Ten Years Later

Lou Wise

"I'm 33 for a moment
Still the man, but you see I'm a "they"
A kid on the way, babe.
A family on my mind"

-----Five for Fighting

13 TEN YEAR RECAP

Welcome to book two, the second half of *Wise or Otherwise*. In case you missed the really big letters on the last page, this part of the book takes place roughly ten years after the first part.

So where do I begin? Well in the spirit of Book One, pour yourself a *"**Drink**"* (You will need it). I think I will start with the here and now and work my way back to how I got here. If that's ok with you. If that's not ok with you well tough shit, you are so far into this book you won't stop now. I know the feeling, my editor says the say the same thing to keep me writing.

There comes a time in every man's life that he must grow up. A man must one day leave the childish ways of getting drunk every night, sleeping with anything that has a pulse, pouring whiskey on his cereal. There comes a time to understand, to reach out and touch tomorrow, to take the future in hand. To see a new horizon, one built on things we have done, not the mess that lays in our wake. To persevere through the joy and the tears, to discover all that this wonderful world has to offer. To move through life with the courage that the years have brought us.

To embrace morality, spirituality; the good pure life. To find a good job, work hard, provide for others. To give to charity, volunteer your time, save the planet. To find that right woman, to marry her, to raise a family. This time will one day come to every man.

One day a man looks to the future and must decide the ultimate course of his life. Will you be a knight in shining armor, who rides in on your white horse and sweeps the waiting damsel off her feet? Will you ride off into the glorious sunset, hastened on your way by the smell of wildflowers and the chirping of friendly woodland creatures? Every man has deep inside him the yearning to set free his inner hero, "Prince Charming" if you will. When a man truly loves a woman he would live for her, die for her.

To quote the illustrious Michael Bolton:

> *"When a man loves a woman*
> *Can't keep his mind on nothin' else*
> *He'd trade the whole world*
> *For a good thing he's found"*

A good woman is the glue that holds a man's life together. She loves him, supports him, comforts him in his time of need. Those classic marriage vows are classic for a reason. This may come off as drivel but this is solid, time tested, sound advice. If you, as a man, can always put the needs of your wife, your queen, above your own, you are already ahead of the game. Marriage is a sacred, honored establishment that will increase the quality of your life exponentially.

So when this time of your life approaches... Run like hell! It is the stupidest fucking idea on the planet. How do I know? I'll tell you. I did it. I got married to one of the most evil women the world has ever seen. I can see Lizzie Borden sitting in hell pointing up at my ex-wife saying, "Damn! That's a cold Bitch!"

So now, right now, I am finishing this book drinking a glass of vodka, yes straight vodka, while my two sons sleep upstairs. Yes, you read that right, I now have two sons... and yes, as previously mentioned, I did get married. But don't lose faith in me yet. I waited till way after they were born to marry the love of my, no that's not right, that special person meant for, no, how do I describe her? I know, that crazy bitch they call mom. Well, before I spend the next couple of pages destroying my ex-wife let me tell you a bit about what has happened in the last decade. I could fill an entire book with stories about her evilness. As a matter of fact, I think I will; buy that one too.

Lou Wise

"It's astounding
Time is fleeting
Madness takes it's toll...
But listen closely...
Not for very much longer..."
----- Rocky Horror Picture Show

14 Ten Years Later

So yes, it has taken me the better part of a decade to write this. No, I really haven't spent ten years writing this. It was more like twenty minutes ten years ago and twenty minutes now. Plus the amounts of scotch and vodka that I have drank. (It takes a while to ***"Drink"*** as much as I have, about ten years in fact.)

The second part of this book may sound a bit different; it may have a different tone. The reason for this is that over the last ten years not only have I grown up but also my editor changed.

Gone are the days of Grec. He is now a big something or other for the publishing company; in his place is a woman editor.

61

Now, I don't believe that this is a bad thing. Especially when the woman is hot (Yes, I am a pig), and mine is. I have done well over the last ten years and would only agree to a new editor if: one, I am apparently under contract, (So I have to write or pay back the advance money) and two, if she's good editor (She is)....and hot. The problem arises when you write things ten years ago and you don't remember how offensive you actually were.

Here is a piece of advice for everyone: when you make fun of the guy who doesn't drink, the guy who wears a towel around his neck, or when you repeatedly say that girls who have tats and piercings are easy (which they are), make sure your next boss or editor isn't a women who has piercings and tattoos. It may make them mad. Forget the "may" part; it will piss them off. I have a really bad feeling that my lovely, wonderful, and the exception to the piercing/tattoo rule editor is going to insert a really bad, untrue story about me. (Did I kiss enough ass there... I hope so.)

Also, as a guy, it is hard working with a chick editor. When I was with a woman hating male editor I could say just about anything I wanted. Now I fear that when I say things like "Her vagina looked like a dollar store ham and cheese sandwich that has been left in the sun on the dashboard of your car for five hours" she may edit it out. (Ha, Ha, you can't edit that out; it is an example, not a reference.)

The point of the last story is that I want my readers to know that I have not lost my edge... I am now being EDITED. And I am pretty sure I have pissed her off. "Her" being my editor. Imagine you have worked your way into a publishing company, you have done the grunt work and are waiting for your big chance. When your big chance turns out to be this book, you must hate life. I feel bad for my editor. Not bad enough that I won't randomly throw in a sexist, offensive comment just for fun. But I understand how pissed she may be.

Imagine going into the publishing industry and hoping to edit Stephen King, James Patterson, the late Gardner McKay, and Vince Flynn. And at the end of the day, you get me. Holy crap how much does your life suck right now?

Oh shit, did I really just call her out on that? Yea, I guess somewhere in this book there will be a story that's not actually my own... SHE is probably going to insert some embarrassing, wildly untrue, but hilarious tale about me...

Here's a fun and unusual story for you to enjoy. When Lou, I mean I, get really drunk, I mean absolutely shit-housed, falling down drunk I have a penchant for dressing up in the clothing my ex-wife left in my closet. I particularly love her satiny undergarments and long, flowing dresses. Even though ~~Lou's~~ my feet are much too big to fit comfortably, wearing her stiletto heels makes me feel like such a desirable, attractive lady, and they accentuate ~~Lou's~~ my better than average, dare I say excellent, posture. I'm quite proud of my physique and my snappy way of dressing, whether I'm wearing my business suit or slipping into something a little more comfortable. Sometimes when I've had a really stressful day at the office, when ~~editing~~ writing all this drivel has me wanting to tear my hair out (I know ~~you're~~ I'm not Stephen King, but Jesus Christ, really?!) I like to drink some Chablis, slip on a little black dress, go out at night and really paint the town. I know I can count on you Constant Reader (All 17 of you) to keep my sexual proclivities our dirty little secret. I'm not saying that Lou, I mean I, always get dolled up on the weekends and go out trolling for strange men while wearing my fanciest come hither outfit, but I'm not *saying that he I don't either. As a matter of fact, I'll be getting my drink on this weekend at Dr. Frank-N-Furter's Transylvania, an illustrious and well known destination for cross dressers, time-warpers, and freakshows (especially ones who like to insult their editor.) It's located at the corner of I Wear Women's Underwear Ave. and I Sometimes Suck Huge Dicks Blvd. Did I already mention that there is a direct correlation between the way a man carries himself (think of your favorite snappy dressing, well postured author) and his potential for blowing a strange man in a dark alley behind a nightclub while wearing a Victoria's Secret (Don't sue me!) push-up? Well, there is! It's almost as much of a certainty as the fact that when you say women with tattoos and piercings are easy, and your editor is a pierced and tattooed woman, you'll end up with an embarrassing and (probably) untrue story inserted into your book without your knowledge.*

"These boots are made for walking, and that's just what they'll do one of these days these boots are gonna walk all over you."
-----Nancy Sinatra

15 WORKING WITH A WOMAN

Working with a woman is not *always* a bad thing. (I wonder how many people I just pissed off with that one sentence?) It is true though, going from a male editor to a female editor has been a huge change but a beneficial one.

Talking about my female editor... I will say it has been a very stimulating experience. We have at times had a meeting of the minds. Together we can get the creative juices flowing. It's not always easy being my editor. (Hell, I drove my last one to drink way more than he already did.) I can't spell, use grammar correctly, and I use monosyllabic words. I guess I do know how to stimulate her thesaurus though.

Editors have it nice though. She can spout off whenever she feels like... Me, I have to wait at least till she spouts off for a paragraph or two (she prefers three) before I can even get a word in edgewise. If I start spouting off before her, let's just say I am in trouble.

And after she spouts off, she likes to lay it all out there...

Lay it ALL out there

The hardest part of writing this is after a few sessions of writing she says, "I can do this all night". Damn lady, I can only type so much.

All the grammar rules suck... Put a semi colon here but not there... Very frustrating. Sometimes I really want to put it where it doesn't belong. I'll make it fit; I do what I want. I don't have to make it fit, it fits all by itself and it feels sooo goooood. I mean putting a comma there just feels right to me.

I don't mean to talk negative about her all the time. Sometimes she really has to bend over backwards to accommodate me. She can be quite flexible at times.

And I don't really want to, but she is making me wrap it up. I will finish a chapter the natural way the way it feels right. The way I want. Actually, she is right I should wrap it up.

Speaking of finishing, finishing is the hardest part... You start a chapter in one place but where do you end? It is usually an argument. Do you take her advice at face value, or do you just fire it in there and hope that nine months from now you don't regret it?

(For those of you who are not that good at innuendoes or who have been playing along with the drinking game part of this book, go back and read the last few pages. This time though, as you read know that every time I mention a literary term I am talking about sex. ie "Put your *comma* where? Makes more sense now doesn't it?)

"Well, he must o' thought that is quite a joke
And it got a lot of laughs from a' lots of folk,
It seems I had to fight my whole life through.
Some gal would giggle and I'd get red
And some guy'd laugh and I'd bust his head,
I tell ya, life ain't easy for a boy named "Sue.""
-----Johnny Cash

16 NAMES

I have learned over the years that a person's name matters. We all know that our last name gives us a sense of belonging, makes us feel connected. Some of you may be able to trace your family name back hundreds of years; ladies when you take your husband's last name (and you should take it, none of this hyphen crap), it shows your devotion to him and the family that the two of you hope to create. Last names are important.

As important as last names are, first names are as important as the last name if not more important. Parents I hate to tell you that there are gender specific names. Please don't name a boy Courtney, Lauren, or Sally. It is embarrassing and not cute. The same is true for girls.

Do not give a girl a boy name. Guys, if you date a girl with a boy's name never call her it. Make up a cute feminine nickname for her. Let me explain why. You're sitting at the bar with a couple of buddies talking about what you did last night:

Guy 1 "I watched a good game last night."
Guy 2 " I took my wife out to dinner."
Guy 3 " I had a crap day at work, went to bed early."
You " I fucked Charlie in the ass last night."

At that moment the table goes silent. Hopefully no one at the table is named Charlie, because if they are you most likely just got punched.

Ok I hear you, that may be a bit extreme so maybe you simply say, "I fucked Charlie last night." or "I had sex with Charlie last night." or "I went down on Charlie last night." or "Charlie was blowing me while we watched the game." Or, well you get the point, this story doesn't end well for you.

So maybe you can talk your way out of it with your friends. Think about your neighbors; you leave the window open one night and they hear you yell "Oh yea Charlie, harder!" or "Faster Charlie faster!" or "I love that thing you do with your tongue Charlie." And you wonder why you get odd looks from your neighbors while mowing the lawn.

To continue on about names, parents please, I beg of you, spell your kids name correctly. What do I mean by this? Don't get creative with the fucking spelling. "Chawn" is not "Shawn", Em'millie" is not " Emily".

The reason our kids can't read isn't because of video games or too much television, it's because their name defies every law of phonics. Name your kid "Chawn", pronounce it Shawn, and you wonder why he can't read. He spent the first five years of his life believing that "ch" makes the sound of an "s". Fuck, the kid is doomed. Give the kid a fighting chance. Would it really kill you to have used an "s"?

..."the pleasure was worth all the pain"
------ Jimmy Buffett

17 SEX PART TWO

"Drink" So as I have previously mentioned this book
takes place ten years after the first. Also as I have previously
stated, I have learned a lot. One area where I have definitely
gained experience is in women and sex. At least, I think I have
gained experience there.

Before you think I am some sort of braggart who is just
making up stories about his conquests, I will prove to you that I
am the real deal. I was once voted "Most Mediocre Man
2010," by a very respectable though small magazine in the
mountains of Upstate New York.

Having received this honor, I understand the pressures
that come with these awards. Once you win "Most Mediocre
Man 2010" you feel the need to behave in a sexy way all the
time. I don't agree with these awards personally. In fact, I find
these awards tantamount to body fascism.

Though the last few paragraphs were complete bullshit I

still do have some useful advice for you.

Here is my first piece of advice: date older women. Please don't get me wrong when I say older. I don't mean older as in a strong wind will cause her to fall over and break her hip. Nor do I mean that you can take advantage of her AARP discount when you and grandma go to dinner and order the early bird special. (If you want to get home in time to watch Murder, She Wrote you have to eat early. Just sayin'.) I'm not referring to your old cash cow type of broad. When the milk is curdled is it still a cow or a fromager? (That's a person who makes cheese... Love my Word of the Day calendar!) What I'm trying to say here is I don't mean a ninety year old lady, though she could use the walker as support. (Think about it.) I mean a girl with experience.

Yes guys, we all have that fantasy of the hot, young, 18 year old virgin chick. That's fun don't get me wrong, but what do they really know about sex? Not much.

They know how to look cute and lie down. Though you can brag to your friends that you banged a young chick and they may give you a high five, was it really that good?

Cute and young only goes only so far. Experience and talent... now that is a whole nother story. Plus they may be little and cute now, but they will grow bigger and well, bigger. What are you going to do, marry her? Now she grows bigger, older, and bitchier, takes you to court and takes you for everything you are worth.

Explain this to your friends. Tell them "Remember five years ago when I said I had a hot little eighteen year old chick? Well, we got married, she "grew," had a kid and divorced me... now fifty percent of my income goes to her... Wasn't I so cool back then?"

(Guys, this is the time of life called payback...)

Compare that eighteen year old to a woman who is older and knows what she wants. When the woman says, "Next time I come over, I am bringing duct tape. The only problem is that mmmrrrmr, is gonna have to be the safe word." or " I bring the duct tape, you bring the mop and bucket..." (When you need a mop after sex, you know you had a good time. Notice the multiple periods hint, hint.) That is hot. When a girl says "I will do whatever you want." and means *whatever you want,* you know you are in for a good night. (And probably a good morning, and even mid-afternoon.)

The next morning when you wake up, do you want to tell your friends about it or do you want to call out of work for the next round?

Here is my definitive rule about how to judge how good the sex was: If you want to tell your friends and brag... not good. If you are willing to call out of work to go for another round, which at this point is probably going to be pushing double digits, now that is good sex. Plus, think about the bragging rights then... no, don't. Chances are if it was that good, you won't even want to admit to your co-workers what you just did. (Think about it. *"Drink"*)

Guys and girls, take this next story as a word of warning. A beautiful singing voice can be sexy, alluring and very attractive. The magical sound of a person's voice may draw you to them like no other, but beware. In the singer's mind they are saying "Oh I use my voice to make pretty sounds... I must be good in bed." You will hear their sultry tone and think, "Oh they use their voice to make pretty sounds...they must be good in bed."

That is so not true. Why? How can that be, you ask? Because if you have ever had sex with a bird, you will know it is so disgusting, and they make pretty sounds with their mouths as well.

Guys, you know we will lie our asses off to get sex. Girls, you know guys will lie their asses off to get sex, so don't seem all that surprised when you catch us in one. Why do I say this? Well beyond it being true and everyone knowing it; the problem is that girls want to believe the guy's lies and if they find out they are not true, well, they will be pissed. It's a game.

Having said this, guys, you must be smart about your lies. Here are some of the major downfalls that I have found with guys lying to get sex.

First, guys, please don't talk about how big your dick is... they know you are lying. (Every guy does it, they know.) Also if they ever ask how big it is, don't say eight inches, everyone says eight inches. (It's a wonder that we could ever build

71

anything when everyone's definitions of eight inches are so
different.)

If you say eight inches, they immediately think
"Bullshit!" And they are right. None of us are exactly eight
inches, we may be more or less but not the standard response of
eight. So don't fucking say it!

Use the real number if you, like me, are slightly bigger.
Say eight and a half, eight and three quarters, anything but
eight even. If you are under eight inches, (sorry) you need
come up with a snappy answer.

For example, I know a guy named Elliot. He's a decent
guy, reasonably attractive, but kind of a little fellow. His
standard line when discussing his attributes (or lack thereof)
with potential carnal mates is "I'm hung like a light switch. It's
exactly the same on as it is off." It always gets a chuckle and
usually ends with the girl needing to find out for herself if such
an outrageous claim can possibly be true.

Guys please, girls will know if you lie about your size.
They have all seen a ruler a few times in their lives.

I have to admit it, girls have a leg up on us with this one.
We judge girls on breast size. You can ask a girl the size of her
breast and she could lie completely to your face and you would
never know. I wouldn't recommend flat out asking a girl about
the size of her breasts. You're more likely to get the shit
slapped out of you than to get an actual answer, be it the truth
or a lie.

Guys do you really know the difference between a "C"
and a "D" cup? Be honest, we judge on a very simple scale:
small, medium, and large. I know, I over-simplify that, we
actually have other criteria; perky or saggy, lactating or not,
and most importantly how quickly they will show them to us.
(So not lying, would you rather a pair of "D's" that you will
never see or some lactating "A's" that are right in your face? I
thought so.)

Moving away from sexual organs, let's talk about our life
situations. This is another area that guys shouldn't lie about,
it's really easy to get caught. Don't tell a girl that you have a
mansion on the beach when you don't. She is going to be
thinking, "Why does he want to go to my place when he has an

awesome house?" If you still (and you have my sympathies) live with your parents, I understand. So will they; times are hard.

Don't tell a woman you are divorced when you are not, the wedding band leaves a mark and tan line.

Also, if you try and play the sympathy card, get it right. I once heard a guy tell a girl that "One day he hopes to be a widower". Reread that last sentence, and then I will set the scene. This guy, we will call him Ed, has not had the best luck with women. Ed has tried all the other stories: "I have money," he doesn't. "I have an eight inch dick," he doesn't. He was desperate. He concocted this big story about how he was married, she passed, and he was alone and scared. He hoped he could find some girl who would take sympathy on him and basically sleep with him to get his confidence back and to make the world right again.

Not a bad tactic, I have seen it used before and actually work. As pathetic as it is, it *could* have worked. But unfortunately for Ed, he fucked up his prose.
Ed told this very sympathetic girl that "One day he wanted to be a widower" instead of he "was a widower".

Screwing up that phrase doomed him. In a matter of a few seconds, he went from sad and pathetic potential pity fuck to creepy serial killer.

Lou Wise

"You wake up late for school man you just don't wanna go. You ask your mom, "Please?" but she still says , "No!""

-----Beastie Boys

18 KIDS

Since becoming a father, I have come to the realization that I have no idea how I survived this long. I don't mean because of the drinking, smoking or rough sex; I mean how did I ever survive childhood?

One reason for this is I know now that if I sleep wrong, say arm tucked under me the wrong way, on too soft of a mattress, on the bathroom floor, the next few days I feel it. My back hurts, my hips ache, my head feels like it's going to split open like an over-ripe cantaloupe every time one of my thing might be because of the booze and not my age.) Kids, they children shrieks, "Dad!" (Although that last don't feel a thing.

Imagine this: while I'm writing this chapter, my kids are blowing bubbles in the driveway. My three year old starts chasing the bubbles trying to pop them and in doing so runs head first into the door of my car. He doesn't put his hands out to stop himself, he simply uses his forehead as brakes. He hits the car so hard he leaves a small dent.

I see this and expect a trip to the emergency room. He sees it differently. He bounces off the car, looks at me, a little stunned mind you, then runs off to chase the next bubble.

What the fuck? Had that have been my head hitting the door this book would have ended at the last chapter. I would not have recovered from that.

I have seen kids do the craziest shit and bounce right back. I know the things I do now (and pay the physical price for), had I have done them at their age I would have been fine.

The other reason that I am so surprised that I made it out of childhood is not for the things I did to myself, but for the things I did to others. How did my parents not kill me. I know that there are times that every parent wants to choke the life out of their child.

Now I know, I normally put lists at the *end* of books, but I will make an exception here. Here is a list of all the reasons that parents would be justified for taking out their kid. Kids: listen very carefully. Parents: you may want to hang this on the fridge.

1. DVD's are not Frisbees.
2. The DVD player is not a receptacle for the peanut butter and jelly sandwich you no longer want.
3. Nor are daddy's DVD's that he keeps in his sock drawer suitable for you to watch.
4. 3am is the time the bars close... not a time to play.
5. 3am is not a time to come in my bed and pee. (Yes, I'm blaming it on you.)
6. Also, 3am is not the time to want a sandwich that will eventually end up in my DVD player.
7. Don't ask daddy's female friends if they are going to have a sleep over.
8. When you walk into any store it is not suddenly time

to go to the bathroom.

9. Same goes with when we just pulled out of the driveway. That's why I asked you if you had to pee before we left the house.

10. Speaking of peeing, don't piss in the bath tub…

11. But if you have to release a bodily fluid in the tub please pee, don't take a crap…

12. Seriously, don't take a crap in the tub.

13. Any white powder you find under the sink or in Daddy's sock drawer is not for you.

14. You have homework… I know it, you know it. (I tried the same lie when I was in school.)

15. I won't lie to you. You can play with it all you want without going blind or growing hair on your palms… But seriously, don't do it at the dinner table or while sitting next to me or next to a priest. (Especially not next to a priest!)

Lou Wise

*"I'm freaking out, where am I now, I'm upside down,
and I can't stop it now…"*
----- Avril Lavine

19 I KNOW I AM IN LOVE

As you get older, love gets very complicated. Now I have to warn my readers that this chapter may not be filled with many jokes. (It will probably be but I think I still need the disclaimer.) I, for once in this book, am writing from the heart, not the bottle. (Actually, without the bottle I would never have written this.) Please don't skip this chapter, it will be worth it.

I know at the beginning of book two that I started all sappy and that was on purpose. I made you read two pages of drivel for one joke. (Sorry about that, but I hadn't written in ten years and I thought it would be funny.) This chapter is not leading to a great joke, at least not at this point. I need to be serious for a moment. I, for once, will write what I want because I want to write it.

I have been unknowingly in love with a women for years. I say unknowingly because I loved her but something wasn't right. Now it is.

I know I said, "When you think it's time to grow up, blah blah, blah… run like hell," and that still rings true. But if you didn't heed my advice, you have by now learned a very valuable lesson. In learning that lesson, the next time you find yourself in a similar position, you will know if it is real or not (read: pre-nup or not).

If you haven't figured out by now that since my marriage ended I have dated a few (lot) of women and had a bit (lot) of fun, then you really need to put this book down. I have dated, slept with, hung out with lots of women since my marriage. I liked so many of them for so many different reasons.

I was happy "dating" them for a time but I never had a vested interest. After the failure and pain of my first marriage, I was looking out for only three people: my two sons and me. I had no intention of ever bringing another person into their lives. I dated women that they (my sons and the other women) never knew about. But one day you run into THAT girl.

I now realize that "THAT" girl was the girl from chapter 10. (Go back and read it.)

Done/ Good. You now see how I felt about her ten years ago.

You, my dear and precious few readers, I have to tell you how scary this is. I am not scared of much, not to this point. I am not scared of not having sex, (it sucks not having it, but well yes, it's a bit scary). I am not really that scared of physical harm, but this girl I am scared of.

Now don't take that as I am scared she is going to hurt me, (she will not turn me into freshly ground coffee in the freezer), or that I am scared that she will ruin my reputation (this book will do that without anyone's help); I am scared to lose her.

I am so scared to lose her that I won't commit to her. I would rather keep the little that we have for as long as possible than push for the whole thing. What is worse: having everything for a period of time or part forever? If only someone would have said it more eloquently, something like "it is better to have loved and lost then to never have..". Fuck it, no one would ever say something like that. It's so lame.

Let me take step back for a moment, and explain how I,

how we, got here. Our relationship started ten years ago.
There was a lot in common, but I would say in all honesty that
it was purely sexual. Well hold on, not purely; there was
always something else there, at the time I didn't know what,
but something.

At the time, we were both more or less single but led very
different lives. Today we still live different lives but our values
are more inline. We both have kids. She a daughter, me two
boys. Our priorities have changed a bit.

Now, don't misunderstand me, our desires are still the
same, (duct tape) but we also value new things. Nothing makes
me happier than to watch her be a wonderful mom to her
daughter. As I write this she is singing her daughter a lullaby.
Yes, her voice is amazing, she defies the bird sex theory.
(Damn! I tried to keep this serious.)

Before you my precious few readers go and say I sold out
for the "kid card", I, well I partially did. I love her (crap, said it
again) but not just for her motherly instincts. She is still more
than a few years younger than I, hot as hell, and has the same
raw sexual passion that I knew ten years ago. Plus,
"mmmrrrrm" is her safe word of choice.

Guys, when you find that woman who doesn't remind you
of your sociopathic ex, likes to drink as much as you even if it's
still before noon, loves her child and your children as well, is
willing to let you do things to her that I can't even write about
because if I did it would preclude my book from being
published, but was still interested in snuggling... You found the
one!

Real quick story, we go out and get drunk. I mean real
drunk, blackout drunk, like we needed bandages from the walk
home drunk. We go to bed, get naked and fall asleep. I have to
be at work in a few hours, she has nothing to do this day. I get
up, try to be quiet, get showered and dressed, but as I am
leaving she rolls over and says, "Kiss me before you leave."
Best kiss ever.

I have finally realized why I wrote this book in the first
place. Besides the alcohol, the pressure from Grec, I needed a
release. I needed an outlet for getting over a girl. Yes, sad, but
very true. I just didn't realize at the time which girl it really

was. Now I know, and because of that I have my muse for the second part. (Did I just really write all that?) ***"Drink"***

"Did you say your name was Ramblin Rose?
Ramble on baby, settle down easy…"
-----Grateful Dead

20 DRUNKEN RAMBLINGS

I have included this chapter as a collection of random thoughts. By thoughts, I mean things that I have done and have gotten an adverse reaction to from people I have told these situations about. So I present them to you here; I will let you be the judge of "Is it that bad?"

Is it that bad if your girlfriend invites you to her house to have a threesome with her and her sister, your girlfriend passes out, and you have sex with the sister anyway?

Is it that bad if you get dumped and spend every waking moment trying to get her back? And when that doesn't work you spend every waking moment trying to better yourself so as to show her up and show her what she is missing?

Is it that bad to allow your girlfriend to talk you into having a foursome with your best friend's girl and your best friend's girls sister? Shit, I hope not.

Is it that bad to just flat out ask a girl when she is gonna blow you? You go, Matt!

Is it that bad if your friends confide all of their personal, private, and embarrassing stories to you, and you put them in a book so you can profit? (Heh, heh, heh)

"...So just give me beer til they get here
Yeah I know the sun is coming up
And ya'll are probably getting ready for closing up..."
-----Rehab

21 IN CLOSING

So what was the point of this book? Fuck if I know. If I could have summed this book up in a few sentences, I would have. It would have been way less work for me and you would not feel like you have just wasted a few hours of your life. (Although you may not feel as if your time was wasted if you have been playing along and *you* are wasted. *"**Drink**"*)

I will, though, try to sum up the point of this book.

First, life is unpredictable. You have to roll with the punches. Did I want to be a raging alcoholic? Well, actually yes, but that's not the point. I am, so I deal with it. Did I want to be a single dad in my thirties? No, but I wouldn't change it for the world.

Second, enjoy life. I don't mean just yell, "Fuck it all!"

85

and see what happens. I've tried that and it usually ends up with a man in uniform reading me my rights. Or a man in a fake uniform doing bad things to me.

Third, love sucks. Not really, love is an amazing thing. Unfortunately, it ends in pain. Not the good pain that includes duct tape and safe words, but real, heartfelt pain. In the end though, it is worth it. But I will say, if you do plan on getting married, I have two words you should always remember... Pre Nup!

Next, I'd like to apologize for disgracing the written language. Thousands of years ago man developed the written word; I think if he knew that someday it would be used in this respect, he wouldn't have. So, to those who came before me, I apologize.

Culpability for this literary crime is shared with the authors friends, and publisher. Please direct all complaints to those people, not me. All threats of lawsuits should be addressed to my attorneys. The law offices of Dewey, Screwum, and Howe.

Yes, save your breath, I know I'm going to hell for writing this book. But hopefully it sells enough copies, that I can afford an air conditioned seat while I'm down there. Perhaps a skybox, or one near the stage.

So, you bastards better have enjoyed this book. I am going to pay dearly with my friends, with history, and perhaps The Almighty. Hopefully he finds this humorous. I doubt it though.

Plus, my mom is gonna read this. How embarrassing. "Here mom, I wrote a book." "What's it about?" " Well let me see... Sex, drinking, let me rephrase that, vulgar sex, my alcoholism,, and a bunch of other shit." She will be so proud of me.

"Just give me a reason
Just a little bit's enough"
-----Pink

22 THE LIST

So, I realized at the end of this book I had a lot more words of advice, more knowledge that I needed to impart on you. Unfortunately, I was not creative enough to turn these bits of wisdom into a good story. So, I took the easy way out and made a list.

1) Do not get drunk and talk to other people's girlfriends. Though fun, it will usually get you hit.

2) Do not stick your fingers in cigar cutters when you're drunk just because someone said, "Hey, stick your finger in here." This one really needs no explanation. It will, though, explain all the typos in this book.

3) Do not ride a bike on the ice or slick snow when you have a thorn patch at the end of your driveway. This one will undoubtedly confuses all of my readers from those warmer climates down south, so let me explain. Ice and snow are slippery. Thus, you skid on your bike, fall, and impale your tender, frozen skin on some frozen solid, razor sharp thorns.

Not cool.

4) Despite what we all like to think, not EVERYTHING is smokable.

4) Despite what we all like to think, not EVERYTHING is smokable.

5) Don't get stoned and repeat yourself.

6) Don't throw Frisbee's at lit light bulbs.

7) Eating a one pound block of cheese is not a good idea.

8) Don't take pills just because they are there.

9) Don't get drunk and run around naked at a shopping center. Wait, forget that one. Running around naked in a shopping center is actually kind of fun (until the cops show up and the next thing you know, you have to register as a sex offender each time you move.)

10) Yes, gasoline smells good, but don't smell it for too long.

11) Check the expiration date on orange juice before making shooters.

12) No, you will never be able to clean up all the glass after throwing plates off of the balcony.

13) It is not smart to dance on the roof, despite the thrill.

14) Most cats have claws. So, don't blow in their faces just because they make a funny face.

15) Avoid animals when on ecstasy. Animals fight back.

16) REALLY avoid trees when on ecstasy. Splinters hurt. Plus, it is really hard to explain to your doctor how you got splinters "down there."

17) If they are hot and drunk, they probably have a boyfriend that is big and drunk. Once again, you may get hit. But in this case, you may also get laid. The decision is yours my friend.

18) Watch who you make the "that person is running like a Jew in Poland '45" crack in front of.

19) If you see a homeless guy that looks like he's dead, don't try to wake him up. He probably is dead.

20) Don't laugh at him either. It's not that cool to laugh at the dead.

21) Just because they are wearing sunglasses doesn't mean they are blind.

22) Empty paintball guns + old people = probation.

23) Don't hit shopping carts with your car, as fun as it may seem.

24) No, it's not fun to get drunk and hit your drunk friend in the face with a champagne cork.

25) Do not burn things in the bathroom.

26) Although making Dale Earnhardt death jokes can be quite amusing, do not make them to large, burly truck drivers.

27) A pellet gun CAN kill a dog

28) Once again I need to stress not getting drunk and hitting on your friend's girlfriend.

29) Don't show up at your friend's house with a bottle of Jack Daniels in your hand without calling first, sometimes their parents are home. Unless, of course, your friend is out and his hot mom is there.

30) Think about this when you're a pedestrian: "No, that car probably can't see me coming from around the corner."

31) Paint thinner is very flammable. Don't smoke and huff at the same time. Trust me, it takes a while for eyebrows to grow back.

32) "Hey, let's just dump the gas directly from the can into the burn barrel!"...No, don't do that either.

33) No cops believe, "We were just going to Hardee's" at 2 am.

34) Getting blitzed and knocking on random people's doors at 11 pm may result in an angry man confronting you with a pistol.

35) The first place your parents look for weed is your top drawer.

36) And, as good of a hiding place as it may sound, the second place they look is above the door frame inside of your closet.

37) Yes, those goofy fake wrestling moves really do hurt.

38) That girl's parents WERE serious about "No cum stains in my car or I'm gonna bust your nose." They meant that. Really!

39) Yes, even if it's a mom saying it.

40) Don't tempt drunk friends to "Spray me with that mace, I fucking dare you." Because they are plastered, and they will.

41) Your parents don't really believe that you're using that lighter for candles and incense.

42) Those floor fans in your room are moving faster than you think, even if you're tripping, (especially if you're tripping.) The cover is there for a reason.

43) If you work at a fast food place and someone pulls up to the drive through acting all cocky, don't spit in their food, give it to them, and say, "Fuck off, goat fucker" under your breath because they may be your grandparents.

44) Girls know you're not bending down underneath your desk JUST to get your pencil...

45) Just IGNORE those people who are selling you knock-off Gucci handbags in the Baltimore subways. Don't get pissy with them, they probably have knives.

46) A pellet gun can go through shoe leather too, you know...

47) This isn't TV, the bottles don't break on people's heads. They give them concussions

48) The first time you have a sexual encounter with a woman, make sure you can see what you're doing. The small one's probably the asshole.

49) Sticking your dick in the vacuum cleaner hurts

50) Warm apple pie does not feel like pussy

.

Wise or Otherwise

AKNOWLEDGEMENTS

I would like to thank first, my family. I hope you never read this book, it's kind of vulgar and weird, but I love you guys. Thank you for all your support over the years.

Next, I would like to thank all my friends. You guys have put up with my shit for years, and you still call and hang out. I would especially like to thank those of you who have let me tell your stories in this book; even those of you who had no idea that they were ever going to be published. Sorry, guys.

Here is a list of people would like to thank, I have used initials so as not to embarrass them. Hopefully I have remembered everyone. First, the brothers I never had B.F., M.E. and C.P. Hey C.P., I know you're away eating sand and kicking ass for us. Thank you, and all those who serve next to you. You are the reason that I was able to write this. God bless, and Godspeed to you all. Happy hunting.

To the people whose stories I "stole" for this book, B.Hudson., J.B, A.G., and T.O'm. and to the girls who inspired many of the stories in the book; S.M., N.L, S.H., K.G., A.Z, D.E., S.B., J.O., L.M.,. P.S.- Most if not all of the people whose stories I have borrowed have given verbal/ signed consent for me to use them. I love my friends.

Next, I would like to thank some people publicly. First, my publisher, Al Greco. This drunk had the faith in me to keep pushing me, to force me to put the effort in and to finally finish this book. Thank you Grec.

For those of you who like this book, you can thank Grec for pushing me, for supporting me, for making this all possible. For those of you who didn't like this book, blame Grec. He made me do it.

Nancy Prevatt, thank you for being my editor. I believe that you have done a great job on this book. Grec thinks highly of you and that is enough for me. I hope your name being associated with this book doesn't end your career.

To Katie Blalock, I don't know how to thank you for your help. Honestly, Nancy and I would never have been able to meet our deadline without your help and this book would have been infinitely worse, (if that is at all possible). I know your career is just starting. I truly apologize that the first time you'll ever see your name in print is in this book.